3 SECOND **SUCCESS**

3 SECOND **SUCCESS**

HOW TO **MASTER MOTIVATION** IN **3 SECONDS!**

SMASH YOUR GOALS,

UNLEASH YOUR POTENTIAL

AND FEEL FULFILLED

EDWIN ARMSTRONG

3SECOND**SUCCESS**.COM

Paperback   ISBN: 978-1-913705-00-8
eBook   ISBN: 978-1-913705-01-5

Author: Edwin Armstrong
EdwinArmstrong.com

Publisher: Acorn Oak Books
AcornOakBooks.com

! WARNING !

URGENT

You are in direct danger of living a life that ends up with you never ever having what you want in life.

MISSION

Get motivated.

Be successful.

Feel fulfilled.

INSTRUCTIONS

3. Get motivated fast with 3 Second Success.

2. Follow the easy to execute steps.

1. Build your Success Window.

GO! Live the life you want!

PREFACE

Which moment will change your life?

Life changing moments. We all have them.

Here is the brief story of mine.

I was 28 years old. This was my life:

- Seriously out of shape.

- Working a dead-end job.

- Living in the city's worst neighborhood.

- No direction in life.

- No goals or ambitions.

- Failed English and Math in high school.

- No savings.

- Living paycheck to paycheck.

Life looked bleak.

Struggled to motivate myself to even do the basics in life.

I knew that I was capable of so much more than this.

I could feel it inside me.

Where do I even start?

Mind completely blank. I had no idea.

I looked back at life and found something that I was good at.

During high school I played sports.

My sport was basketball.

I decided to watch some videos of basketball and came across a clip of Michael Jordan that I remembered watching over and over as I grew up.

It's May 7th, 1989.

It's the NBA playoffs.

Michael Jordan's team, the Chicago Bulls, are losing the game by 1 point.

There are 3 seconds left in the game.

With 3 seconds to go Michael Jordan takes action. He sprints up to the free throw line. Right before the buzzer he takes a shot.

He scores!

His team, the Chicago Bulls, win the game!

With only 3 seconds left in the game what is the point in trying?

Most people would have given up. He could have given up.

He didn't. He still gave it everything he had.

In his mind he was going to win the game.

He did win the game.

This got me thinking about playing basketball when I was younger.

There is a rule called the 3 Second Rule, also known as 3 in the Key.

Under the basket there is a painted zone area called the key. As a player, if you enter this zone you have 3 seconds to take action or your window of opportunity closes. 3-2-1. If you don't take action and you're still in the key, it's a foul. You either take action or lose the opportunity.

Playing basketball when I was younger, I had an inspiring yet tough coach. My coach, Jim, used to do these practice drills where you had the ball in the key against multiple defenders.

He would shout out:

3-2-1-GO!

On GO! you had to take the shot. No excuses. You took the shot no matter what.

His explanation was that if you don't take the shot you are guaranteed to lose. You are right next to the basket why not take the shot anyway? You could score. You could miss, get the rebound and take another shot. You could miss and the other team get the ball, but smart players still gain from this. Even if you miss you learned about your opponents. You gained experience to make the next shot easier.

I have 3 seconds.

What's it going to be?

Lose or win?

That was the moment that changed my life. I realized that for years I had just been standing there in the key. Letting opportunity after opportunity slip by me because I was not taking action. We all have our zones of potential linked to our goals. Just like the painted zone under the basket.

In these Action Moments we have 3 seconds to take the shot. To smash our goals. To unleash our potential. To be successful.

After 3 seconds the window of opportunity closes. If we take action and take the shot, we always score. We make progress and we succeed.

I made this my life principle.

I started using it all day every day.

Whenever I had life and work goals, I imagined I was on the basketball court.

I had 3 seconds.

The basket was open.

I can score.

All I had to do was take the shot.

Just take the shot.

3-2-1-GO! and on GO! I took the shot.

Shot after shot after shot.

And you know what?
I scored.

Again and again and again.

My life changed fast.

My life changed forever.

Started working out regularly.

Signed up to night school.

Started saving money.

Moved home to the good side of the city.

Got my grades at night school.

Accepted into University.

Quit my dead-end job.

Traveled the world.

Graduated University: First-Class Degree with Honors.

Successfully started businesses.

Successful investor in stocks and real estate.

I went from being a nobody with nothing to building the life I want.

All because of 3 simple seconds.

It's time for you to get the life you want.

3-2-1-GO!

Edwin Armstrong

May, 2020

P.S.

Thank you, Michael and Jim.

Because of you guys, I got what I want in life.

CONTENTS

CONTENTS

YOU

"YOU **MISS 100%** OF THE SHOTS YOU **DON'T TAKE**"

WAYNE GRETZKY

SUCCESS

Do you know what you're truly capable of?

Deep down inside you know. You feel it. When you were a child you proudly said what you would be when you grew up. You were motivated and had ambitions. Ambitions that you were certain you would make real.

Where did that motivation go?

You aren't alone. Every day millions live their lives as robots. Wake up, work, sleep. Repeat and repeat and repeat forever. Look around you. Everyone forgets their true potential and keeps it buried deep down inside them. What a waste. The #1 regret at the end of people's lives is not living the life they wanted because they were afraid of taking opportunities.

3 Second Success transforms your entire life. We will dig out and unleash your true potential. Enjoy living your new life of success!

OPPORTUNITY

To truly understand opportunity and success we're going to experience them.

Sit up straight.
Roll your shoulders back.
Open your chest.
Breathe deeply.
Smile and smile big.

Think of a positive time when you took an opportunity that resulted in success. Close your eyes for a few minutes, imagine the success and re-live it as if you were there right now.

How do you feel? Speechless.

It's such a powerful feeling that words can't describe the feeling of success. Do you want to feel this success feeling every day? Learn how with 3 Second Success.

Every day there are windows of opportunity popping open all over the place yet most of these windows slam shut with the opportunity passing you by. Think back over the past year. How many opportunities did you miss?

Imagine what would be different about you and your life now if you had acted on those opportunities.

These windows of opportunity have a domino effect. When you act on one window of opportunity another window opens and so on, before you know it you've multiplied the first opportunity 10-fold just by acting on the windows of opportunity as they open.

Imagine where those missed opportunities from the past year could have taken you.

Let's look at how one simple window of opportunity could completely change your life.

WINDOW OF OPPORTUNITY: WORKOUT

You're a member of your local gym but struggle to find the time to go regularly. You go past the gym on the way home from work and they're offering half price personal training if you sign up this week.

NORMAL YOU

You've had a long day at work and think to yourself "I'm too busy and tired now, I'll do it next year".

1 YEAR LATER

You still can't find the time or energy to go to the gym even though you're a paying member!

ACTION YOU

You've had a long day at work and think to yourself "Great offer, I'm going to do this" and go into the gym. You sign up for the personal training at 2 sessions a week for 3 months with a personal trainer who is full of energy. Their positive attitude is so inspiring that you eat a healthy dinner and get to bed early that night. The next day you wake up feeling refreshed and can't wait until your first training session. Your personal trainer takes their job seriously, they run through your sleep pattern and diet in addition to your workout and create a plan for the next few months. You stick to the plan and after 3 months you feel so amazing that you sign up for the rest of the year.

1 YEAR LATER

You stand in front of the mirror at home and are blown away by the progress you've made. Your physique is beyond what you thought possible. It was challenging but you stuck with your diet, sleep and workout plan. You look great and feel great. Because you feel great your inner confidence is massively boosted. You made new friends at the gym and one gym friend asked you to join their team at a local sports club. You took the opportunity, joined the team and made new friends there.

RESULT

Acting during those few moments of the first window of opportunity resulted in multiple follow on windows of opportunity opening. You got in shape, changed to a healthy diet, got the sleep you need, boosted your confidence and made a bunch of new friends. All because of that first window of opportunity and the domino effect of the following windows of opportunity.

WINDOW OF OPPORTUNITY: WORK

You get an email first thing in the morning at work which says that they're looking for a volunteer to lead a new project with the deadline for volunteering being the end of the day. In the weekly meeting after lunch the project will be discussed and anyone who wants to volunteer should send a short application email.

NORMAL YOU

You've got a backlog of work to catch up with and the weekly meeting is usually a waste of time. You think to yourself "I'll skip the meeting and I'll spend that time catching up on work, maybe I'll volunteer next time".

1 YEAR LATER

You're still catching up on work, it feels like it never ends!

ACTION YOU

You've got a backlog of work to catch up with and the weekly meeting is usually a waste of time. You hit reply to the email saying that you're interested. A colleague noticed you send your email and mentions that their old manager did a similar project before, they'll see if they're free over lunch for a quick chat. You speak with your clients and colleagues to check their deadlines and they're happy to wait a few more days, your work isn't as urgent as you'd thought. You have a quick chat over lunch, this person is a goldmine of information and they're happy to help further down the line. You go to the meeting after lunch, this time there's a few important people there who talk about the project. You contribute and ask some great questions that they show interest in. You send your application email and get selected as the project leader.

1 YEAR LATER

The project went great and over the course of the project you became friends with your colleagues' old manager. It went so great that you were offered a promotion and pay raise to a job that is heading in the direction of your career ambitions. You took the opportunity and are enjoying the new job. You get on well with your new colleagues and are in line for a further pay raise at the end of the year. With the extra cash you've been on vacation and are looking at moving to a new house.

RESULT

Acting during those few moments of the first window of opportunity resulted in multiple follow on windows of opportunity opening. You got to lead an exciting project, made new friends and colleagues, got a promotion, moved your career forward in the direction you wanted, boosted your income, went on vacation and have the money to move to a new house. All because of that first window of opportunity and the domino effect of the following windows of opportunity.

WINDOW OF OPPORTUNITY: BUSINESS

You've got a unique idea for a business, no one else is doing this yet and it has huge potential. You tell your friend and they say they know someone who's an investor and can set you up with a meeting.

NORMAL YOU

You haven't worked out the details yet and need a business plan. You tell your friend "I'll work out the details and let you know when I'm ready". You're busy. Developing the business idea is what you want to do but it always seems to get pushed out of the way by urgent work and family responsibilities.

1 YEAR LATER

You're almost started on the business plan. You're going to do it next week. Really, this time it will get started next week!

ACTION YOU

You haven't worked out the details yet and need a business plan. You tell your friend "Great, thanks!" and invite them both over to watch the game at your place on Sunday and talk business. On Sunday you, your friend and the investor bounce ideas around. The investor likes your idea and needs more information on the details. You agree to meet up in a month to run through the details and the investor tells you exactly what to research, where to get the information and how to prepare your business plan and investor pitch. The investor wants you to pitch the idea to them just like all the other businesses they deal with would have to.

1 YEAR LATER

You're sat at your desk and lean back with a smile on your face. You look around at the small team you've built and feel confident about the next phase of the business. You think back to frantically working all hours to get your business plan and pitch finished, how nervous you were when delivering it and how waiting for the investor's final confirmation felt like an eternity. Over the past year you've learned more than you did in the past decade. Quitting work was easier than you thought and there's no going back now. You were offered an office in a great location at a discount rate through an old acquaintance who heard you were starting a business. The business is on track and the financial goals are looking like they will be realized earlier than expected. Leading the business is both demanding and rewarding at the same time with looking forward to going to work being a perk that you'll never get tired of.

RESULT

Acting during those few moments of the first window of opportunity resulted in multiple follow on windows of opportunity opening. You secured funding for your business, escaped from your normal job, learnt a bunch of business skills in months, set up an office, hired a team, enjoy going to work at your new business and are on track to financial success. All because of that first window of opportunity and the domino effect of the following windows of opportunity.

TRUTH

Look in the mirror. Get up, go to the mirror and look at yourself. Stare yourself directly in the eyes. You are looking at the only person holding you back and the only person who can drive you forward. You and you alone define your success. Windows of opportunity present themselves daily, yet we lack the strength and confidence to act and these opportunities pass us by.

3 Second Success is a powerful tool that is proven to work. It works by motivating you to take action fast. You have the potential inside you waiting to be released. 3 Second Success will empower you to unleash your true potential and enrich your life. Get ready, you're about to step on the accelerator and pull into the fast lane of success!

3 SECOND SUCCESS

"DREAMS BECOME REALITY WHEN

INTENTIONS BECOME ACTIONS"

ANCIENT PROVERB

WHAT IT IS

3 Second Success is an easy to use motivational tool that instantly and permanently changes our normal default behavior across all areas of our lives.

Built on solid scientific research this metacognition tool allows us to take control of our own brains to change from inaction to strong and confident action that results in success after success.

Start doing things that we want to do by motivating ourselves to change the habit of inaction to the habit of action.

As we've seen, windows of opportunity pop open all the time. We normally hesitate and persuade ourselves that we'll do it next time, but next time never comes. This hesitation creates a moment for our brain to persuade us to take the easy route of inaction.

What if there was a way to transform these inaction moments to action moments? Let's learn how!

INSTRUCTIONS

STEP 1:
ACTION MOMENTS

When we want to take action towards a goal but feel ourselves hesitating, we have only a few moments to change from inaction to action. Recognize these Action Moments and become aware of them.

STEP 2:
3-2-1-GO!

In an Action Moment count down:

3-2-1-GO!

On GO! move and take action!

POWERFUL

The simplicity of 3 Second Success is what makes it so powerful. It empowers us to unleash our full potential in every situation throughout our lives.

ACTION MOMENTS

Teaching ourselves to recognize Action Moments makes us aware of all the windows of opportunities that pop open and present themselves daily.

COUNTDOWN

Counting down 3-2-1 during an action moment commits us to focusing on our goal by preventing us from hesitating and being distracted by overthinking, fears and worries.

TAKE ACTION

Moving and taking action on GO! drives us forward towards our goal and success.

PRACTICE SUCCESS

Practice makes perfect. Start small and start using 3 Second Success every day. This practice deletes our old default inaction habit and replaces it with a new action habit. Building this new habit is important for unleashing it when it really counts. Through practice we will change our default behavior from inaction to action with life changing consequences.

Start now. Look around, what housework needs doing? What has been sitting on our to do list forever?

Need to do the dishes after dinner?
3-2-1-GO!

Pile of clothes to wash?
3-2-1-GO!

Trash needs taking out?
3-2-1-GO!

Home messy and needs tidying?
3-2-1-GO!

Practicing every day trains our brain to take advantage of Action Moments. This training builds a new habit. With this new habit when windows of opportunity pop open, we'll automatically 3-2-1-GO! to success!

WHEN TO USE

It feels great to use 3 Second Success to get things done that have been waiting for months! We're now ready to take 3 Second Success outside and unleash our potential on the world.

When can we use 3 Second Success? Any time that we feel an Action Moment. The moment we feel that we want to take action towards a goal start counting down:

3-2-1-GO!

On GO! move and take action! Be creative, use 3 Second Success everywhere and start enjoying the results.

In this book we will learn, with clear step by step instructions, exactly how to use 3 Second Success to achieve:

STRENGTH:	**BE STRONG**
CONFIDENCE:	**BE RESPECTED**
OPPORTUNITY:	**BE SUCCESSFUL**

WHY IT WORKS

PROBLEM

We want to do something, we know we should do it, but we persuade ourselves to either do something else instead or wait until the future.

We want to go to the gym, we know we should go but it'll be OK if we skip today, go next week and sit down to watch TV for a few hours. Next week is always next week and after a year our gym shoes still look like new because they've never been used.

We deserve a pay raise at work, we know we should ask for one, but it'll be better if we wait until next month when we're up to date with all our work and then ask. Next month is always next month and after a year our pay is still the same because we never get up to date with work so don't ask for a pay raise.

We choose the easy option or wait for the perfect time. We persuade ourselves that this is the best decision. The reality is that before we know it, our default behavior is inaction and every time a window of opportunity pops open it slams shut instantly. This leads to life goals never being realized, feelings of low self-esteem and feeling guilty because we know we can do better.

SCIENCE

Neuroscience has proven there to be clear reasons for this inaction behavior with the root cause of inaction being our unconscious brains striving to keep us alive and safe. Our brains are trying to help us but in our modern reality, they hold us back.

ENERGY

Energy in the form of food is needed by our bodies to sustain our metabolism and drive our muscles, energy keeps us alive.

Our ancient ancestors evolved in a harsh environment where food was hard to come by and the next meal was never guaranteed. Saving energy kept our bodies ticking over until the next meal to increase our chances of survival. We evolved an instinct to avoid unnecessary physical exertion in order to conserve calories. This instinct to save energy is why we wait 5 minutes for the elevator to go up 1 floor when we could have taken the stairs in 10 seconds and why we watch TV instead of going to the gym.

STRESS

Stress is a feeling of strain or pressure such as when we do something new that is unfamiliar and daunting or something risky that could fail.

Our ancient ancestors evolved in a harsh environment where danger was everywhere. Stress is like radar that helps us avoid danger to increase our chances of survival. If we needed to go out of our cave and hunt for food but there were lions roaming around, we'd put off getting food and distract ourselves by finding a nice corner to do a few cave paintings until it was safer. We evolved an instinct to want to escape stress or at least find a distraction and shelter from the stress. This instinct to escape stress is why we distract ourselves with browsing the internet instead of facing the stress of starting work and why we distract ourselves with trying to get up to date with work instead of facing the stress of asking our manager for a pay raise.

BRAIN

When faced with a decision, task, action or situation our brains start up in this order:

1st: INSTINCT
2nd: RATIONAL THINKING

This is why when we're put on the spot, we go blank, but a few minutes later we're overflowing with ideas. On the spot our brains engage instinct first to deal with saving energy and avoiding stress but nothing else which leaves our minds completely blank as our rational thinking hasn't been engaged yet. Once our instincts determine that we're not wasting energy and we're safe from stress our brains shift from instinct mode to engage rational thinking mode which is when the ideas start flowing. Our ancient ancestors were kept safe by evolution using instinct first then rational thinking later. When faced with life or death decisions we needed to act instantly to stay alive, there wasn't any time to sit and think about our options when a hungry lion jumped out on us. In modern life we've all had something scare us and instantly, before we can think, our heart is pounding in our chest and we can feel the adrenaline pumping making us hyper alert. This instinct, known as the fight, flight or freeze response, is a clear example of instinct kicking in before we can think. The instinct to hesitate and take the easy option of passing up on an opportunity is another clear example that we all experience. The same process of instinct first then rational thinking second happens when we're faced with any decision, task, action or situation. Our brains use instinct first to save energy and avoid stress then thinks rationally second.

There are different areas of the brain that support instinct and rational thinking. The limbic system is an area of the brain that supports instinct, this controls our energy saving and stress avoidance instincts along with other instinctual behavior. The frontal lobe is an area of the brain that supports rational thinking, this controls our logical decision making along with other cognitive behavior. Brain scans conducted by cognitive neuroscientists have shown that during a variety of decision-making tasks key structures of the limbic system are activated first with specific structures of the frontal lobe activating second. Our brains helped our ancestors survive but in the modern world our brains hold us back.

SOLUTION

Our brains act on instinct to save energy and avoid stress only for survival right now in the present moment, when in instinct mode we're not thinking about the future benefits that we'll enjoy from achieving our goals. Instinct mode doesn't realize that going to the gym will make us healthier, instinct mode only understands that we'll be using energy at the gym and we need to avoid using energy unnecessarily. Instinct mode doesn't realize that asking for a pay raise will allow us to go on vacation, get a new car and get a new house, instinct mode only understands that asking our manager for anything is stressful and we need to avoid stress. This is often interpreted as laziness, a lack of ambition or a lack of motivation. Everyone experiences this because this is how our brains are wired to work, instinct first then rational thinking second. We're not lazy, lacking ambition or lacking motivation, we just need a way to engage our rational thinking first and take action fast before our instincts persuade us otherwise.

When we're hesitating to take action towards a goal how can we:

Activate rational thinking?
Take action fast?

COUNTDOWN

Numbers are processed using the rational thinking area of our brains. Starting to count instantly activates our rational thinking and because counting uses a series of numbers it delays our instinct mode from activating by keeping our rational thinking mode engaged.

Now that we're counting, and we've activated our rational thinking we need a way to take action fast before our instinct mode has chance to activate and take over. The longer we count for the more time our instinct mode has chance to activate, by keeping our countdown as short as possible at 3 seconds we focus on taking action towards our goal. If we count forwards 1-2-3, we can keep counting forever and it doesn't work. When we count backwards 3-2-1 we have nowhere to go after "1" which provides a direct prompt to take action.

MOTIVATOR

Having a motivator that drives us to take instant action is vital. "Go" is the prime action word, it's short and direct which drives us to take action instantly.

3 SECOND SUCCESS

Combine the countdown and the motivator and we have 3 Second Success. A simple, memorable, fast and powerful tool to overcome the everyday problems of hesitation and inaction that we all face which result in life goals never being realized, feelings of low self-esteem and feeling guilty because we know we can do better.

3-2-1-GO!

Now, we can do better, we can be confident, and we can realize our life goals by transforming our intentions into actions through using the proven power of 3 Second Success.

CHANGE YOUR LIFE

AUTOMATE

3 Second Success opens up a new world of opportunity. Learning how to use this tool effectively will maximize your potential to enjoy success after success. Windows of opportunity pop open all day every day and pass us by because of the way our brains are wired to work. Using 3 Second Success to overcome our instincts when we feel an Action Moment is simple and easy. However, there are many windows of opportunity that pop open where we don't consciously realize that they're even there and then they slam shut in seconds without us being able to take action as we didn't feel the Action Moment. It's only later that we realize there was an Action Moment and we wish that we had taken action. How can we automatically recognize Action Moments and use 3 Second Success instantly without even thinking about it?

HABIT

Habits are subconscious routines of behavior that are repeated regularly. We all have loads of habits, common ones are brushing our teeth in the morning and locking the door behind us when we leave home. We complete these actions automatically without thinking and often don't realize that we're doing them. Have you ever gone back to check if you've locked the door? We all have, this is because we were on habit autopilot when we locked the door and didn't even realize we had done it.

Habits are governed by a neurological loop known as the habit loop. The habit loop consists of 3 elements:

Trigger: Anything that starts the habit
Routine: Behavior of the habit
Reward: Benefit from the habit

In the morning, the moment we step into the bathroom is the trigger, the routine is to grab our toothbrush and start brushing our teeth and the reward is a clean and fresh mouth. When we leave home, the moment we close the door is the trigger, the routine is to lock the door and the reward is a safe home whilst we're out.

Habits are formed through practice and regularly repeating the routine behavior. Over time the routine behavior becomes automatic, when we experience a trigger, we automatically start the habit. Habits take time to form, the time it takes varies with the type of habit that we're trying to form and our personality. On average a habit takes 66 days to go from being something that takes conscious action to being automatic action, but this can vary depending on our individual personality to anywhere from 18 days to 90 days. If we want to form a new habit the sure way to do this is to use 90 days or 3 months.

SUCCESS HABIT

Habits automate our behavior and actions when we experience a trigger. We can form a new success habit to automatically use 3 Second Success without even thinking to maximize our success. To ensure that we establish this success habit we will use 3 Second Success at every Action Moment we experience over the next 3 months. Every Action Moment where we want to take action start counting 3-2-1-GO! to move and take action. From small Action Moments like tidying up or choosing a healthy lunch to big Action Moments like starting our own business, every Action Moment where we use 3 Second Success builds our new success habit. The elements of this success habit:

Trigger: **ACTION MOMENT**
Routine: **3-2-1-GO!**
Reward: **SUCCESS**

At any time, the moment we want to take action is the trigger. 3-2-1-GO! then move and take action is the routine and the reward is the feeling of success in working towards and completing our goals.

To make this success habit an automatic habit we will do this for 90 days or 3 months. Set a reminder on our smartphones for every breakfast, lunch and dinner time every day for the next 3 months that simply says:

3-2-1-GO!

Do it now, get out our smartphones and set the reminder before we read any further!

Every day for the next 3 months, every time that we're eating the reminder pops up. This will keep us on track and build our success habit fast.

As we use 3 Second Success more and more, we will start noticing more and more windows of opportunity and Action Moments that would previously have passed us by without us realizing. Use 3-2-1-GO! to move and take action to take advantage of these new opportunities and enjoy the feeling of success after success.

BOOST

Boost our success even further with 2 simple things that will grow and grow our results, a journal and planning for future opportunities.

JOURNAL

A journal only takes minutes to write and massively boosts our success. At the end of every day whilst in bed, note down the following 3 simple things:

Journal Date: 1st May

<u>SUCCESS</u>
1 opportunity we took today.

<u>MISSED</u>
1 opportunity we missed today.

<u>TOMORROW</u>
1 opportunity we will take tomorrow.

In the morning, read what was written. Keep it short and to the point, like this:

Journal Date: 1ˢᵗ May

<u>SUCCESS</u>
Woke up on time and got out of bed

<u>MISSED</u>
Watched TV instead of going for a walk

<u>TOMORROW</u>
Chicken salad lunch, not usual snacks

Write more detail if needed and write for ourselves, don't worry about what we write, spelling or grammar. This journal is for us to record our progress and motivate ourselves to future success.

Keeping a daily journal is like a time machine, we now have the power to review our past successes and predict the future by planning the opportunities we will take. Reviewing our journal every morning provides accountability to ourselves to take opportunities today. Our journal provides a permanent record of our progress empowering us to review our successes daily and boost our motivation. Building a record of past successes to flick through is a bulletproof way of pushing through difficult times in the future and ensures every day ends with a smile. Realizing and recording missed opportunities drives us to take those opportunities next time they come around and enjoy success.

3-2-1-GO! get 2 simple notebooks. Put a notebook next to the bed and start a journal today, save the other notebook for planning.

Every night when going to bed make it a habit to 3-2-1-GO! for the journal and make notes. Every morning make it a habit to 3-2-1-GO! for the journal, read what was written last night and commit to taking that opportunity today.

PLAN

Planning gives us control. Planning puts us in the driver's seat. We get to make the choices and decisions rather than leaving things up to chance or allowing others to make decisions for us.

When we know there will be a window of opportunity in the future we boost the success of this opportunity by planning our actions. It doesn't matter if the future opportunity is in 30 minutes or 6 months, all future opportunities have their success boosted through planning. Planning identifies the Action Moment when we will use 3 Second Success and empowers us to focus our actions on success at that decisive moment.

The plan needs to be simple to be memorable and easy to action. An effective plan uses these 3 core elements:

GOAL

What we want.

ACTION MOMENT

When the window of opportunity opens.
When we start counting down 3-2-1-GO!

ACTION

Actions to get what we want.
The action we take on GO!

Keep it short and to the point for simple goals, like these:

GOAL
Get out of bed on time

ACTION MOMENT
Moment when open eyes
3-2-1-GO!

ACTION
Get out of bed. Go wash face to wake up!

GOAL
Go for a walk after dinner

ACTION MOMENT
Moment when finished eating dinner
3-2-1-GO!

ACTION
Put shoes on, open door and go!

Use detail for more in-depth goals whilst being short and to the point, like this:

GOAL

Work project feedback from colleagues

ACTION MOMENT

Weekly Review Meeting: Moment before the meeting summary starts
3-2-1-GO!

ACTION

Say "Feedback on the project would be great. Let's go through what went well and what we can do better next time"
Discuss and write down feedback

Having a plan is like a road map that guides us to our destination. A road map stops us from getting in our car and driving around aimlessly, hoping to eventually reach our destination. Using a plan is like using a road map, we can see our destination which is our goal, see our starting point as our Action Moment and know exactly where to take turns just the same as taking actions towards our goal.

Planning works best when written down. The action of writing commits our plan to our memory and empowers us to take strong and confident action when the window of opportunity opens whilst we are in the Action Moment. When we know a future opportunity will happen but there isn't enough time to write a plan go ahead and create a plan, a fast plan that isn't written down. Think to ourselves what the goal is, when the Action Moment will be and what action we will take. Go over this fast plan a few times in our head to really remember it. Having this fast plan empowers us to confidently and instantly take advantage of the Action Moment when the window of opportunity pops open.

3-2-1-GO! grab the other notebook and pen, this is now our success planner. Think of a future opportunity coming up. Write down the goal, Action Moment and action. Every time we know about a future opportunity go grab the planner and write down the goal, Action Moment and action. Each time the windows of opportunity pop open our planning provides the power to act with strength and confidence resulting in success after success.

3 SECOND SUCCESS PRO

We've transformed how we think and act using 3 Second Success. We feel amazing, like a new person. It's time to step up our game and go professional.

Lifelong success is achieved through strength, confidence and creating opportunity. These are the 3 pillars of a fulfilling and happy life. We will now go through step by step instructions that detail exactly how to use 3 Second Success to build strength, to build confidence and to create opportunities. Simply follow these easy instructions and we will find our sense of purpose, enjoy happiness and feel fulfilled in life.

STRENGTH:	**BE STRONG**
CONFIDENCE:	**BE RESPECTED**
OPPORTUNITY:	**BE SUCCESSFUL**

SUCCESS WINDOW

All top performers know the importance of picturing themselves succeeding in their minds before they take action in reality. Visualization has become essential in professional sports and business. Regardless of their profession, top performers know that the power of visualization is extremely effective when harnessed and transformed into action.

Visualization works because our subconscious brains want to quickly overcome obstacles that stand between us and our goals. Our subconscious brain activates and actively begins solving how to clear every obstacle and it builds a robust road directly to our goal. Our brain has the same activity when we visualize ourselves doing something as it does when we are physically performing that action. This is a game changer because it greatly increases our confidence and comfort level when taking real action towards our goal.

Visualization is a tool that unleashes powerful performance. We are going to use an enhanced yet easy to use version of this tool to build strength, build confidence and create opportunity.

3-2-1-GO! to the bedroom and stand on the bed. Find a wall in the bedroom that can be cleared to create our Success Window. The ideal wall is the wall that we're looking straight at when we're in bed. If there's pictures up, move them. If it's a wardrobe or the back of a door instead of a wall these will work. Throughout the rest of this book we're going to build a Success Window using the 3 pillars of success:

STRENGTH:	**BE STRONG**
CONFIDENCE:	**BE RESPECTED**
OPPORTUNITY:	**BE SUCCESSFUL**

There are 3 pillars of success and each pillar is built with 3 blocks. We need space on the wall for a 3x3 grid of standard size sheets of paper like this:

Each block represents a strength, confidence or opportunity goal. We can write and draw each block or use a computer and printer to print each block. As we go through each pillar of success there will be clear instructions about how to build our Success Window and what to use to represent our goals. 3-2-1-GO! to **3SecondSuccess**.com now for a printable Success Window template.

Every time we are in the bedroom, we will see our Success Window and subconsciously begin visualizing ourselves achieving our goals. Our subconscious brain will activate and solve how to clear every obstacle then build a robust road directly to our goals. Every morning when we wake up, look at our Success Window. Every night before we write our journal, look at our Success Window. Every time we're in the bedroom, look at our Success Window. The more we look at our Success Window the more our confidence will be boosted and the faster our goals will be realized. Get ready, we're going to unleash our true potential and permanently change our lives forever!

STRENGTH

"A FIRM TREE DOES NOT FEAR THE STORM"

ANCIENT PROVERB

A strong body naturally makes us feel confident. Strong body, strong mind. Strength is the feeling that anything is possible. Strength builds resilience enabling us to bounce back from setbacks and power through to achieve our goals. Physical strength means living longer, sleeping better and looking great. Mental strength means improved decision making, improved memory and feeling on top of the world. Building physical strength automatically builds mental strength empowering us to feel as strong as the firm tree that does not fear the storm.

Our physical bodies are like cars. Our bodies need routine maintenance, clean fuel and a regular drive to maximize performance.

Sleep is the routine maintenance that is essential for our bodies to work. Changing tires, brake pads and wiper blades on a car is like our bodies clearing waste, re-energizing cells and building muscle.

Diet is the clean fuel that is vital for our bodies. Cars run for longer and accelerate faster on clean fuel just like our bodies have more energy and are stronger with a healthy diet.

Exercise is the regular drive that is crucial for our bodies. Cars that are taken out for a regular drive run smoothly, this prevents parts seizing up and breaking just like our bodies stay healthy with regular exercise helping prevent sickness and injuries.

Let's 3-2-1-GO! to superb sleep, a dynamic diet and energizing exercise!

SLEEP

Razor sharp focus. Photographic memory. Refreshed and energetic. Organized and on time. Motivated. Sleep makes all these and more happen.

The Centers for Disease Control and Prevention has called lack of sleep "an epidemic". A sleep study found that 76% of people feel tired most weekdays. The study found that this resulted in feeling groggy, being disorganized, forgetfulness and a lack of motivation. A solid night's sleep is essential for enjoying a life of success.

3: WAKE

Win the morning, win the day. When we wake up early, it eliminates the need to rush in the morning. Our day is started on an optimistic note with the positivity carrying over throughout the entire day. Wake up early, reduce stress and enjoy a successful day.

There are two types of mornings, feeling fresh and still sleepy. On a still sleepy morning the alarm violently punches us out of our dreams into the real world forcing us to groggily get ready for the day wishing we could stay in bed. A feeling fresh morning starts with naturally opening our eyes and looking over at the clock to see that there are still 10 long minutes left to enjoy in bed. We feel well rested, alert and ready for the day ahead.

Being jerked out of deep sleep by our alarm every day isn't good for our health. Being rudely awakened by our alarm causes a grogginess called sleep inertia. This sleep inertia impairs our thinking and functioning for up to 4 hours after our alarm punches us out of our dreams. This happens because we sleep in a series of cycles of light sleep and deep sleep. Each full cycle lasts around 90 minutes. When we wake naturally, we are at the end of a sleep cycle and are ready to wake. When we are punched out of our dreams by an alarm, we are in the middle of a sleep cycle and have interrupted a deep stage of sleep.

The key to waking up early is going to bed at the right time.

2: BED

Early to bed, early to rise. When we go to bed at the right time, we get the sleep we need. We fully recharge overnight waking up feeling refreshed and ready to go. Go to bed at the right time, sleep well and enjoy waking up naturally.

There are two types of evenings, without worries and doing duty. On a doing duty evening there's an endless list of tasks that must be finished before bed. Our eyes are closing on their own, but we slog through and eventually get to bed much later than expected, dreading the alarm going off in a few short hours. A without worries evening has a blank schedule. We watch a movie or read a book before taking a long relaxing bath and going to bed an hour early to gently drift off to sleep.

Doing duty and completing every task before bed isn't good for our health. Going to bed late causes a lack of sleep, doing this night after night and week after week leads to a sleep debt which results in our performance, mood and sleepiness all getting worse and worse. The National Sleep Foundation found that every night we need 5 or 6 sleep cycles to fully recharge. Each sleep cycle is 90 minutes which means we need around 7 and a half to 9 hours of sleep each night to wake up feeling fresh.

The key to going to bed at the right time is a regular sleep schedule.

1: REGULAR

Sleep debt to sleep wealth. Consistency is everything. Go to bed without worries and wake up feeling fresh every day.

Our bodies have an internal clock called our circadian rhythm which regulates our sleep-wake cycle. This internal clock tells our bodies when to wake up and when to go to sleep. Our internal clock runs on a regular schedule, with a regular schedule our bodies know when to sleep soundly and when to wake up naturally. Going to bed and waking up at different times daily throws off our internal clock making our sleep-wake cycle a mess. Our bodies don't know when we should be asleep or when we should be awake. This means when we do finally get to bed, our eyes are wide open, and we can't get to sleep because our bodies don't know what's going on.

GO! SUCCESS WINDOW

Let us sleep for when we wake, we will move mountains. The right amount of sleep and a regular sleep schedule build strength.

7 and a half hours sleep = 5 sleep cycles

Get Ready	Bed	Wake
9:00PM	9:30PM	5:00AM
9:30PM	10:00PM	5:30AM
10:00PM	10:30PM	6:00AM
10:30PM	11:00PM	6:30AM
11:00PM	11:30PM	7:00AM
11:30PM	0:00AM	7:30AM
0:00AM	0:30AM	8:00AM
0:30AM	1:00AM	8:30AM
1:00AM	1:30AM	9:00AM

9 hours sleep = 6 sleep cycles

Get Ready	Bed	Wake
7:30PM	8:00PM	5:00AM
8:00PM	8:30PM	5:30AM
8:30PM	9:00PM	6:00AM
9:00PM	9:30PM	6:30AM
9:30PM	10:00PM	7:00AM
10:00PM	10:30PM	7:30AM
10:30PM	11:00PM	8:00AM
11:00PM	11:30PM	8:30AM
11:30PM	0:00AM	9:00AM

Using the tables on the previous pages find the time that we want to wake up in the "Wake" column. The time to be in bed for lights out is in the "Bed" column and the time to start preparing for bed is in the "Get Ready" column. An example is if 9 hours' sleep is optimal for us and we want to wake up at 6:00AM we will start preparing for bed at 8:30PM and be in bed ready to sleep before 9:00PM.

To create this block for our Success Window simply put the time we want to wake up and the time we want to sleep as large and clear as possible on a sheet of paper like the example on the next page.

3-2-1-GO! stick this block on our Success Window as the 1st block like below.

<u>SUCCESS WINDOW BLOCK #1: SLEEP</u>

6AM

9PM

<u>SUCCESS PLAN: SLEEP</u>

Easily enjoy superb sleep with 3 Second Success and the following sleep success plan.

<u>GOAL</u>
Superb sleep

<u>ACTION MOMENT</u>
Bedtime
3-2-1-GO!

<u>ACTION</u>
Stop whatever is being done
Go to the bathroom and get ready for bed
Go to bed

DIET

Dynamic and in the zone. Lively and fresh. Crystal clear mind. Motivated. Diet makes all these and more happen.

Food has a direct impact on our physical and mental performance. When low on energy we're lethargic, losing focus and short-tempered. Research has proven that the more fruits and vegetables we eat the happier, more engaged and creative we are. A healthy diet is essential for enjoying a life of success.

3: EAT

We are what we eat. Eat well, feel better. Eat well, perform better. We get more work done when we eat well, we meet deadlines and stay focused. Eat well, stay focused and enjoy a successful day.

Meals directly impact our brains and bodies over the following minutes and hours. Skipping breakfast and last-minute lunches lead to derailed days whilst healthy meals create driven days. This happens because our bodies convert everything we eat into glucose. Glucose provides energy to our muscles and brains. When we're low on glucose our bodies are lazy and lethargic whilst our brains can't concentrate and are in a foggy haze.

Our bodies process different foods at different rates. High sugar foods like chocolate release their glucose quickly which boosts our energy fast but then leave us in a slump. High fat foods like cheeseburgers need our digestive system to work extra hard to release their glucose. Our bodies divert energy away from our brains and muscles to do this which is why we feel sleepy after a high fat meal. Healthy foods like fruit and vegetables release their glucose steadily to provide progressive energy that keeps us active and on track.

What we eat is important for success. Using 3 simple principles we can decide if any food is a mighty motivator or a deadly downer. The key to driven days is avoiding deadly downer foods and eating mighty motivator foods.

When we're deciding what to eat use the following 3 easy principles.

Is the food:

3: Not sweet?
2: Not fried?
1: Not processed?
GO! Eat!

If the answer is yes to all we can enjoy the tasty mighty motivator food. Food that is not sweet, not fried and not processed provides progressive energy that keeps us focused, productive and motivated.

2: DRINK

Water is life. Staying hydrated keeps the mind crystal clear. Drink well, think fast and produce real results.

What we drink has a similar impact on our brains and bodies as what we eat. When we drink high sugar drinks, we get a short-term energy high followed by an energy slump that kills our motivation.

A single soft drink can on average has 10 teaspoons of sugar. Fruit juice seems like a great natural alternative, but it's packed with natural sugars that on average are the equivalent of 10 teaspoons of sugar. Although fruit juice is natural it has the same bad effect on our motivation as soft drinks. We would never eat 10 teaspoons of sugar straight yet that's what we do when we drink a single can of soft drink or fruit juice.

The average coffee drinker has 3 teaspoons of sugar in their coffee. The average tea drinker has 2 teaspoons of sugar in their tea. Multiply this by how many cups we drink in a day and the sugar in coffee and tea quickly adds up. If we have 3 cups of coffee that's at least 9 teaspoons of sugar. Watch out for the sneaky sugar that slips into our coffee and tea. Boost motivation with the stimulant effects of caffeine by drinking coffee and tea sugar free. Take the time to savor the flavor and enjoy the taste rather than the sweetness. Avoid adding sugar and we avoid the sugar energy slump that kills motivation.

When choosing what to drink skip the sugar by avoiding deadly downer drinks. Stay motivated by drinking mighty motivator drinks using the following 3 easy principles.

Is the drink:

3: Not a soft drink?
2: Not fruit juice?
1: Free from added sugar?
GO! Drink!

If the answer is yes to all we can enjoy the delicious drink. Drinks that are not a soft drink, not fruit juice and free from added sugar provide hydration that keeps us thinking fast, achieving real results and motivated.

1: REGULAR

Lazy and lethargic to fast and focused. Consistency is everything. Eat and drink regularly to create driven days every day.

Our bodies' internal clock, called our circadian rhythm, regulates our sleep-wake cycle. Our internal clock also regulates our hunger and energy levels. This internal clock tells our bodies when to expect food and when to release energy. During the day we need constant energy. Breakfast, lunch and dinner fuel us throughout the whole day. Breakfast fuels the morning, lunch fuels the afternoon and dinner fuels the evening through to morning. Our internal clock runs on a regular schedule, with a regular schedule our bodies and brains know with certainty when more food is coming and can run at 100% all day as the next meal is guaranteed. Skipping meals and eating at different times throws off our internal clock making our energy levels a mess. Our bodies don't know when the next meal is coming so we go into safe mode to save energy. We slow down. Our bodies conserve energy. Skipping breakfast, lunch or dinner might save minutes but it costs us massively through the following hours and hours of low focus, low productivity and low motivation.

GO! SUCCESS WINDOW

Eat great, drink great, feel great. The right food and drink combined with a regular meal schedule build strength.

Choose mighty motivator foods and drinks using the principles.

Set regular times for breakfast, lunch and dinner. Always eat meals and always stick to these times.

To create this block for our Success Window simply find pictures of our favorite mighty motivator foods and drinks. Put them as large and clear as possible on a sheet of paper like the example on the next page.

3-2-1-GO! stick this block on our Success Window as the 2nd block like below.

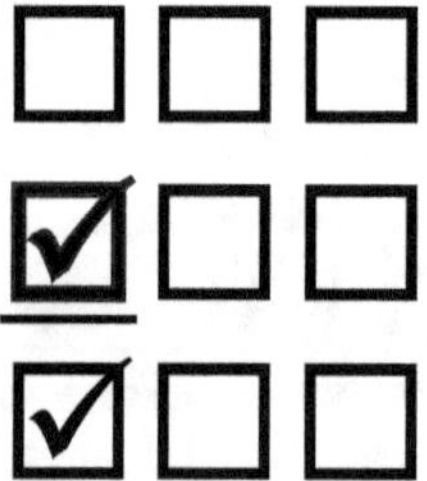

SUCCESS WINDOW BLOCK #2: DIET

SUCCESS PLAN: DIET

Easily enjoy a dynamic diet with 3 Second Success and the following diet success plans.

GOAL
Eat healthily

ACTION MOMENT
Mealtimes:
Breakfast
Lunch
Dinner
3-2-1-GO!

ACTION
Choose what to eat using the principles:
Not sweet
Not fried
Not processed

GOAL
Drink healthily

ACTION MOMENT
When thirsty
3-2-1-GO!

ACTION
Choose what to drink using the principles:
Not a soft drink
Not fruit juice
Free from added sugar

EXERCISE

Determination. Pure power. Invincible stamina. Motivated. Exercise makes all these and more happen.

Exercise builds our bodies. Exercise builds our brains. Regular exercise is proven to reduce fat, build muscle and keep our hearts pumping strong. Exercise not only builds muscle, exercise builds brains. Exercise stimulates the creation of new blood vessels and boosts the creation of new brain cells. Exercise makes our brains grow new cells faster and helps our brains get the energy they need through increased blood flow. This results in increased learning, memory and cognition which translates to us being both physically and mentally strong. Exercise makes us resilient, adaptable and powerful. Regular exercise is essential for enjoying a life of success.

3: STRENGTH

Strong body, strong mind. Building muscle builds self-control, discipline, and drive. A strong body reflects we worked hard for it. A strong body shows patience, work ethic and self-respect.

On average we spend over 9 hours a day sitting. Our muscles waste away because they don't get used. We move from bed to car to work to car to sofa to bed. Every day. This quickly becomes normal and before we know it years disappear following this routine. Our physique goes from solid to soft. We struggle to move furniture and carry shopping. This significantly impacts our confidence, drive and motivation. Build muscle and build strength, everything now feels effortless and easy.

Our bodies build muscle through strength training. After lifting weights our muscles regenerate and grow so that next time it's easier. Muscle growth takes time, this dedication in building muscle also builds our mind. Sticking with a regular weightlifting schedule takes self-control, discipline and drive. These all transfer out to other areas of our lives to boost confidence and drive motivation.

Maximize strength gains by training correctly. Everybody is unique, we all need a personalized work out program to suit our schedule, specific body and strength training goals. Getting a personal trainer and working with a knowledgeable strength training specialist helps prevent injury and boosts results. Self-training works when we use tried and tested methods. Decide what your target physique is. It could be anything from a shredded martial artist to a pumped body builder. Work with a personal trainer who has that physique or use a workout plan that has proven results to get our target physique. Be strong by using the following 7 easy principles.

FORM: Learn to do each exercise correctly. This prevents injury and makes sure the correct muscles are being targeted. Effective strength training depends on proper technique.

RANGE OF MOTION: The load on muscles is greater when using a full range of motion. This increases the strength and size of muscle faster.

BREATHE: Keep breathing. Breathe out when lifting the weight, breathe in when lowering the weight.

WEIGHT: Focus on form first. Add weight later. Start with practicing the exercise without any weight. Get the form, range of motion and breathing 100% correct before adding weight.

BALANCE: Work all major muscles. Legs, core, back, chest, arms and shoulders. Strengthen opposing muscles in a balanced way, such as the biceps and triceps for the back and front of the arms.

REST: Muscles need time to recover, repair and grow. Leave at least 2 rest days between training the same muscles.

REGULAR: Strength train a minimum of 2 times a week. Every week.

2: STRETCH

Stretch for strength. Flexibility training enables full range of motion and optimal mobility. Stretching maximizes muscle strength and muscle growth through more effective workouts.

On average we spend over 9 hours a day sitting and we spend all night sleeping. Sitting and lying in bed don't do much for our flexibility. The rest of the time our lifestyles aren't active enough to promote flexibility. Put simply, we don't move our bodies enough to truly stretch ourselves. Without regular movement our joints get stiff and our muscles become tight. This restricts flexibility, decreases our range of motion and drops our mobility.

A squat is a fundamental movement. To maximize the strength gains from a squat we need full range of movement. For most of us our hip and ankle flexibility limit us and don't allow us to squat deep. Through stretching we can fix this. We can squat deep, lift big and maximize strength gains.

Work with a personal trainer or use a proven stretching plan to boost your strength training success with regular and targeted stretching. Be flexible by using the following 3 easy principles.

SLOW: Ease into the stretch slowly. This allows us to easily find our limit and prevents injury through overstretching.

CONTROL: Keep the stretch and the tension in the muscle under control. It should be mild enough that the tightness disappears after holding the stretch for 30 seconds.

REGULAR: Stretch daily to see effective results. This loosens muscles up and increases range of movement. Turn tense and tight into relaxed and ready.

1: STAMINA

Epic endurance. Go for miles and miles. Stamina training turns our body into an efficient machine.

Living in the modern world means that we rarely break a sweat. Taking the car instead of walking, taking the elevator instead of the stairs and ordering online instead of going to the store all add up to never exerting ourselves. Our bodies have it easy. Our hearts are resting all the time. Our muscles are resting all the time. This adds up to a body that gets out of breath with a thumping heart just tackling some stairs.

Strength training by lifting weights builds muscle. Muscle needs a regular supply of blood to grow. To maximize muscle growth, we need a strong circulatory system that can deliver. Use aerobic exercises that get our lungs working and hearts pumping like running and cycling.

Playing sports, from soccer to basketball, is fun. Loads of fun. With regular stamina training next time we want to join a game we can jump straight in and make it look easy. Work with a personal trainer or use a proven stamina training plan to boost strength training success. Be unstoppable by using the following 3 easy principles.

SWEAT: We heat up whilst we're training. Sweating cools us down. Sweating is a signal of stamina building. When we're sweating, we're building endurance.

HEART: A beating heart builds a stronger heart. When we can feel our hearts pumping, we're building endurance.

LUNGS: Rapid breathing means we're pushing our limits. Challenging ourselves to the point that we're out of breath builds endurance.

GO! SUCCESS WINDOW

Let the gains begin. Train like a beast. A regular exercise training program that utilizes weight training, stretching and stamina training builds strength.

Work with a personal trainer or use proven exercise plans to create a weight training, stretching and stamina training program that builds muscle, builds our brains and builds our strength.

Stick to this exercise training program. 3-2-1-GO! to every session feeling like a champion.

To create this block for our Success Window simply find a picture of our target physique and put this picture on a sheet of paper like the example on the next page.

3-2-1-GO! stick this block on our Success Window as the 3rd block like below.

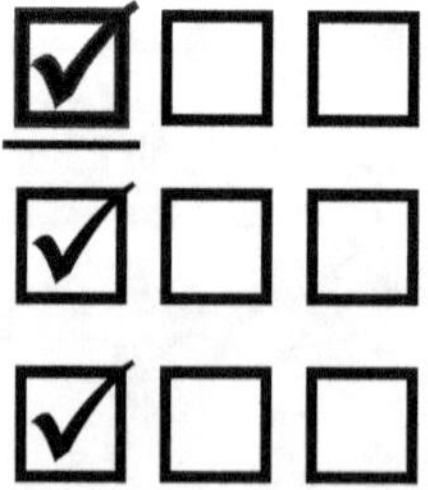

SUCCESS WINDOW BLOCK #3: EXERCISE

SUCCESS PLAN: EXERCISE

Easily enjoy energizing exercise with 3 Second Success and the following success plans.

GOAL
Be strong

ACTION MOMENT
Start of strength workout
3-2-1-GO!

ACTION
Build strength using the following principles:
Form
Range of Motion
Breathe
Weight
Balance
Rest
Regular

GOAL

Be flexible

ACTION MOMENT

Start of stretching workout
3-2-1-GO!

ACTION

Increase flexibility using the following principles:
Slow
Control
Regular

GOAL

Be unstoppable

ACTION MOMENT

Start of stamina workout
3-2-1-GO!

ACTION

Build stamina using the following principles:
Sweat
Heart
Lungs

CONFIDENCE

"THE **MAN** WHO HAS **CONFIDENCE** IN HIMSELF

GAINS THE **CONFIDENCE** OF **OTHERS**"

ANCIENT PROVERB

Confidence creates opportunity and earns respect. Believing in ourselves enables us to rise up and reach our potential. When we believe in ourselves, we are more likely to take action. To stand up and seize the moment. To power through and persevere long after those that doubt themselves. Confidence says yes to opportunity. We set the bar higher, aim higher and achieve higher results. Confidence leads to success. Confident people believe in success and their own ability to succeed. Building confidence in ourselves earns the respect of those around us.

Confidence is like a powerful electro-magnet. Our confidence attracts opportunity, success and respect like a magnet attracts metal. Building confidence is like boosting the power to the magnet to attract more opportunity, more success and more respect.

Let's 3-2-1-GO! to being powerfully positive, truly trustworthy and being with positive people!

POSITIVE

Relaxed and ready. Reaching beyond our comfort zone. Smiling big. Motivated. Being positive makes all these and more happen.

Positive people bring joy, happiness and laughter. Positive people are fun to be around. They bring light and energize their environment. People keep a distance from negative people. People like and gravitate towards positive people. Research has proven that being positive broadens our sense of possibility and opens our minds up to more options. Being positive empowers us to see more windows of opportunity and to seize these opportunities. Being positive is essential for enjoying a life of success.

3: PLAN

Calm and in control. Being prepared saves time and eliminates stress which frees us up to enjoy life. Through planning we are ready for the future and feel true freedom.

Fail to plan, plan to fail. Most people don't plan to fail, they fail to plan. Imagine you are sat in the passenger seat of a car. The driver's seat is empty. You are on a road at the top of a mountain. Your goal is to get to the bottom of the mountain. Sitting in the passenger seat when the car starts rolling is terrifying. The car quickly veers off the road, bumps and rolls down the side of the mountain and crashes before you get anywhere near the bottom of the mountain. Imagine you're now sat in the driver's seat with a road map. The car starts rolling, you steer the car down the road whilst checking the map and road up ahead to get prepared for upcoming bumps and corners. You easily make it to the bottom and had fun along the way. A passenger has no control over where they go and what happens. Without a plan we are a passenger, we get bumped from one surprise to the next and crash before we reach our goals. With a plan we are a driver, we are in control and achieve our goals whilst enjoying the journey. Be a driver, have a plan, be in control. Research has proven that planning reduces stress and significantly increases personal and professional achievements.

Planning is knowing:

WHAT is happening.
WHEN it is happening.
WHO it will include.

Planning maps out our daily, weekly and monthly tasks and activities. Work, grocery shopping and appointments are examples of tasks that we all have. Using a schedule to plan these tasks makes sure that we know what's coming up today, this week and this month. Using a schedule means that instead of being stressed and late everywhere that we're early and ahead of schedule. To start planning we need to record all our tasks on a schedule. This can be an online calendar, a planner notebook or a large wallchart. Choose what works best. Start by planning out the day today. Schedule everything from waking up to going to sleep. Record a start time, end time and who is included for each task. Next, plan tomorrow by scheduling every task that needs doing tomorrow. Keep going until we are at least a week into the future. Every day and week set aside a few minutes to update the schedule for the next day, next week and next month. Planning keeps us relaxed, confident and positive by reducing the chance of failure. We can reduce the chance of failure, but we can never eliminate failure completely. We all will still fail from time to time. How we deal with failure is the key to staying positive.

2: FAIL

Fail big. Failing isn't a step backwards, it's a huge leap forwards to success. Transform failure into opportunity. Fail better and use this unique opportunity to reflect, learn and grow.

The fear of failure is normal. We all experience it. When we're outside our comfort zone we're taking a risk and that is scary. To reach success we must venture beyond our comfort zone into unknown territory where anything can happen. Where anything can happen, we're vulnerable and failure is inevitable.

Basketball players in the NBA on average score 45% of the shots they take. They miss 55% of the time. Professional players always continually fail more times than they succeed. Game after game. Basketball players get paid big money to fail big every game. Let that sink in for a minute. Every player learns from each miss. They learn about themselves, their team, their opponents and the court. They use each failure to increase the chance of success the next time they take a shot. Each failure brings success closer until the game is won. It is impossible to win the game without failing, failing is a crucial part of success. Life is like basketball. Taking a risk is like taking a shot, we win whatever happens. If we score, we win points and achieve our goal. If we miss, we win through learning and increasing our probability of success next time. Either way both outcomes bring us closer to the success of winning the game.

Failure builds resilience and the lessons learned from failure fuel success. This is good. From each failure take away at least one lesson that has been learned. We choose what failure means to us. Choose to fail good. Fail so good that every time you fail it's the best failure yet. The key to continually failing good is transforming failures into learning opportunities by being optimistic.

1: OPTIMISTIC

Believe in better. Optimism is the belief that we can and will take action to change things. Be optimistic. See things as they are. Visualize how they can become better and take action to make them better.

Studies have proven that we react more strongly to negativity than positivity. We dedicate more of our brains to negativity. We remember more negative events in our lives than positive events. When we make decisions, we give a greater weight to negative thoughts. This has been passed on to us by our ancient ancestors whose survival depended on constantly being aware of danger. It was an evolutionary advantage for our ancestors to be cautious and pessimistic, but it stalls our success in the modern world. The media knows this, news agencies fill news reports and bulletins with bad news as they know very well that we pay more attention to them. The world isn't getting worse every day, we see negative headlines because that's what people react to.

Blind optimism is dangerous. This is when people ignore risk to see only sunshine and rainbows everywhere. Ignorance is bliss, but ignorance always catches up. If risks are ignored sooner or later everything cracks and falls.

Being optimistic is about believing in change. Optimism means seeing things as they are by being realistic. Finding both the bad and the good. Next is visualizing how this can be made better. Lastly is taking action to make it better. Using a glass half full of water as an example, as a pessimist we only have half a glass of water instead of a full glass, this is bad. As an optimist we see that there's half a glass of space to put ice in the glass and enjoy a refreshing drink of ice cool water, this is good. Be optimistic, take action and feel good. To be optimistic in any situation use the following 3 easy principles.

BAD: Find what is bad about this.

GOOD: Find what is good about this.

BETTER: Take action to make this better.

GO! SUCCESS WINDOW

Positive is powerful. Planning, failing good and being optimistic motivate continual progress.

Plan days, weeks and months. Feel relaxed and confident knowing what is happening and that we're prepared.

Fail big and fail good. Take away at least one lesson that we've learned from each failure. Learn, adapt and improve. Build resilience and fuel our success.

Be optimistic. In any situation understand what is bad and good then take positive action to make it better.

To create this block for our Success Window simply find a picture that represents being positive and put this picture on a sheet of paper like the example on the next page.

3-2-1-GO! stick this block on our Success Window as the 4th block like below.

SUCCESS WINDOW BLOCK #4: POSITIVE

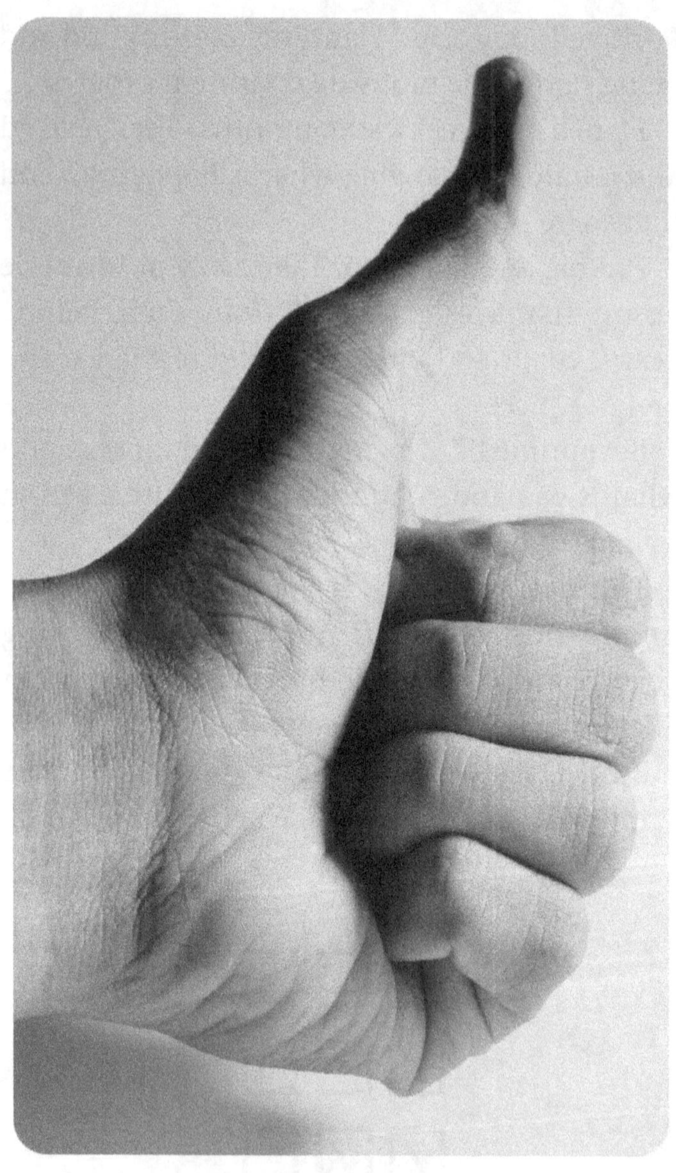

SUCCESS PLAN: POSITIVE

Easily enjoy being powerfully positive with 3 Second Success and the following success plans.

GOAL
Plan and schedule life

ACTION MOMENT
After breakfast
3-2-1-GO!

ACTION
Check and update the schedule with:
What is happening
When it is happening
Who it will include

GOAL
Learn from failure

ACTION MOMENT
When failed
3-2-1-GO!

ACTION
Reflect
Take away lessons learned

GOAL
Be optimistic

ACTION MOMENT
Thinking negatively
3-2-1-GO!

ACTION
Be optimistic using the principles:
Find what is bad about this
Find what is good about this
Take action to make it better

TRUST

Approachably authentic. Friendly and familiar. Self-respect. Motivated. Being trustworthy makes all these and more happen.

Trustworthy people have integrity. They are honest, reliable and dependable. We buy from brands and companies that we trust. We go out of our way to help a trustworthy friend. We can count on trustworthy friends to help us out when we really need it. Inside we are trustworthy. Our friends can count on us when it really matters. On the outside we don't always display our trustworthiness. Studies have proven that people constantly judge others on their appearance and how they interact with others to determine their character. Demonstrating our inner trustworthiness instantly earns the respect of those around us which in turn boosts our own self-respect and confidence. Being trustworthy is essential for enjoying a life of success.

3: LOOKS

Look sharp, be sharp. The clothes we wear change who we are. It changes the value of what we have to say. Look great and build trust through appearance.

Our appearance is like a billboard advertising who we are. Look sloppy and we're advertising that we're a sloppy person. Look sharp and we're advertising that we're a sharp person. The clothes we wear change the way people interact with us. Our clothes subconsciously tell others if we're like them or if we're different. This determines whether they trust or distrust and whether they listen or ignore. What we wear represents the respect we're showing to those around us. Display respect and trust by dressing sharp using the following 3 easy principles.

APPROPRIATE: Wear clothes that are appropriate for the occasion. Consider the location, time of day and people that will be there. What we wear for an important business meeting at the office is very different to what we wear when we're with friends watching a sports game. We've all heard that it's better to be over-dressed than under-dressed. Every occasion will have a spectrum of what's appropriate to wear, always go with the higher end of this spectrum. We can instantly tell if someone has been lazy and thrown on whatever was laying around or if they're prepared and look great. Be prepared, wear appropriate clothes for the occasion and clearly communicate trustworthy confidence.

FIT: Wear clothes that fit. Clothes that fit are like a second skin that float over our bodies. Clothes that are too tight make us feel strangled, they look like we're an adult wearing children's clothes. Clothes that are too loose make us feel lost, they look like we're a child wearing adult's clothes. Most people have been wearing clothes that are too large for them for their entire lives. Lose the loose clothes and find clothes that fit. Clothes that fit enhance our looks by subtly stating we have serious style. Wear clothes that fit and clearly communicate trustworthy confidence.

COLOR: Wear the right colors. Clothing color makes a statement about us and who we are. People use color to subconsciously interpret who we are. Dull colors advertise that we're a boring person. Bright mismatching colors advertise that we're a chaotic person. Avoid colors that clash. Color is a powerful visual stimulator that sends a message without saying a word. Wear colors that complement and balance each other to clearly communicate trustworthy confidence.

2: BODY

Silent strength. Great leaders exude confidence, competence, and trust. Communicate without words by using body language. Demonstrate comfort, confidence and trust.

We're like a book. People around us unconsciously read us all day, every day. We convey who we are and what we are thinking through our non-verbal signals much more powerfully than we do through our words. Our bodies never lie. Just by glancing at someone we know if they're happy or sad. We automatically use their facial expression, posture and movements to read them and build a profile of who they are. This results in a feeling of comfort or discomfort. When we feel comfort, we trust this person, respect them and show interest in them. When we feel discomfort, we distance ourselves from this person. We build trust and respect with others by showing we are comfortable and happy. Clearly convey comfort, confidence and trust with body language using the following 3 simple principles.

RELAX: Being relaxed shows confidence and happiness. It says that we're happy to be here and are enjoying what's happening around us. Stress makes us tense. Our muscles tighten, we project discomfort and everyone around us can feel this. To show that we're confident and happy we relax our whole body. Our face, neck, shoulders, arms, hands, body, legs and feet. Imagine stepping into a hot bath and laying down. All stress instantly disappears, and every muscle instantly relaxes. Loosen up and instantly relax using the thought of relaxing in a hot bath to show comfort, confidence and trust.

SMILE: Smiling is a universal sign that we're happy. Smiling changes our mood, when we smile, we feel better. Smiling is contagious. When someone smiles at us, we smile back. We have a mirroring reaction that causes us to copy the facial expressions we see. When we meet someone who is smiling, we smile, feel happier and enjoy spending time with them. This explains why the more we smile, the more positive reactions we get from others. Our resting face has the power to impact people positively. Having a happy resting face instills feelings of happiness and trust in those around us. Look in the mirror. Relax our face. This is our current resting face. Think of a happy memory and smile whilst thinking about it. As our smile fades pause our smile when our lips are closed and the corners of our mouth are still pointing up. Make this happy face our new resting face with a genuinely authentic smile. Be approachable with a genuine smile to exude comfort, confidence and trust.

POSTURE: A powerful posture displays strength, confidence and trust. Our posture influences how we perceive ourselves and how others perceive us. Bad posture makes us look short, weak and shy. If we look that way, we feel that way. Good posture makes us look strong and confident. Good posture makes us feel strong and confident. Bad posture is a result of small habits gradually getting worse and worse. Working at a desk all day, staring at smart phones and stress all cause our posture to gradually deteriorate over time. Posture involves our whole body. From our feet through our legs, hips, body, shoulders, arms neck and head. Bad posture can involve having a forward neck, hunched back, rounded shoulders, backward tilting hips, leaning on one leg and having our feet too close together. Stand in front of a full-length mirror. Move our feet shoulder width apart with feet pointing slightly outward, like 11AM and 1PM on a clock face. Straight legs with even weight distribution on each leg. Tense the glutes to rotate our hips fully forward, gently release the glutes whilst keeping our hips in the same place. Deep breath in whilst lifting shoulders up and back. Whilst breathing out drop shoulders down and allow arms to hang loosely at sides. Point our head straight ahead so that our chin isn't up or down, just straight ahead. Use 2 fingers on our chin to push our head back and up to straighten our neck. Done. Turn to stand sideways in front of the mirror and do it again. When looking at our posture from the side there should be a straight line going down from our ear through our shoulder, hip and knee to our ankle. Demonstrate strength with a powerful posture to show comfort, confidence and trust.

1: PURPOSE

Slow is smooth. The way we move reveals how we feel inside. Move with deliberate purpose to display calm confidence and trust.

Excessive body movements show nervousness and insecurity. During moments of stress, we tend to practice comforting behaviors like face touching, adjusting of clothes, and tapping our toes. Fidgeting is a clear sign of nervousness. A person who can't keep still, is a person who is worried, tense and not confident. When we're nervous our movements speed up and this can make us look erratic and unstable. Calm and relaxed people don't move unnecessarily. We never see their hands fidgeting or knee bouncing. They move calmly with purpose and are never rushed. Display calm confidence and trust using the following 2 easy principles.

SLOW: Confident people move with purpose by acting at a deliberate and steady pace. Move slowly by pretending that you're in a swimming pool. Moving through water forces you to move slowly. Use this thought when walking and gesturing to move steadily, deliberately and slowly. Slow and natural movements display calm confidence and trust.

LESS: Less is more. Confident people move only when they need to. When you feel the urge to fidget, focus on breathing slowly and deeply to remain calm and relaxed. When talking with people use mirroring or loosen up a bit to avoid being eerily calm by being too still. Mirroring is subtly copying some of their gestures and expressions. Loosen up by expressing yourself using relaxed, calm and open gestures. Deliberate and purposeful movements display calm confidence and trust.

GO! SUCCESS WINDOW

Trust actions, not words. Look sharp, use body language and move with purpose to silently communicate authentic integrity.

Look sharp by wearing appropriate clothes that fit well with colors that truly represent who we are.

Exude confidence using body language by relaxing and smiling with a good posture.

Display calm character using purposeful movements that are slow and deliberate.

To create this block for our Success Window simply find a picture of a person that inspires trust through looking sharp and exuding calm confidence. Put this picture on a sheet of paper like the example on the next page.

3-2-1-GO! stick this block on our Success Window as the 5th block like below.

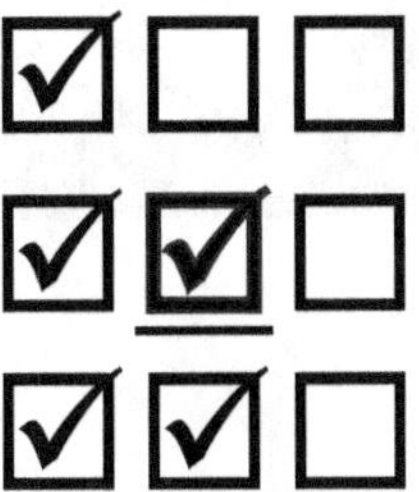

<u>SUCCESS WINDOW BLOCK #5: TRUST</u>

SUCCESS PLAN: TRUST

Easily enjoy being truly trustworthy with 3 Second Success and the following success plans.

GOAL
Look sharp

ACTION MOMENT
Getting dressed
3-2-1-GO!

ACTION
Look sharp using the principles:
Clothes that are appropriate for occasion
Clothes that fit
Colors that are suitable

GOAL

Comfortable and relaxed

ACTION MOMENT

Social interactions
3-2-1-GO!

ACTION

Be comfortable and relaxed using the principles:
Relax: Imagine taking a hot bath
Smile: Happy resting face
Posture: Powerful

GOAL

Purposeful movements

ACTION MOMENT

About to move
3-2-1-GO!

ACTION

Be calmly confident using the principles:
Slow: Like being in water
Less: Deliberate movements

PEOPLE

Challenge and elevate. Value and support. Enthusiasm and learning. Motivated. Being with positive people makes all these and more happen.

Our friends are our future. Studies confirm that who we spend time around has a profound impact on us. We are much more likely to gain weight if just one of our friends gains weight. Friends heavily influence our behavior, both negatively and positively. Our health and happiness are strongly linked to the friends we spend our time with. Real friends will honestly tell us when we're off course, motivate us when we're feeling slow, and inspire great performance when the game is on. We do the same for our friends. We're the average of all the people that surround us. Investing wisely in friendships is essential for enjoying a life of success.

3: LESS

Pro-active protection. Negative people steal our time and energy. Minimize losses by spending less time with negative people.

Negative people are everywhere. At work, the grocery store and even in our own families. We all have these people in our lives. The eternal doubters who are quick to point out when we're wrong. The ones who always explain why our plans won't be successful. The people who bring us down by complaining about whatever's happening in their own lives. They're perpetually negative and bring us down whenever they're around. We allow them to dump garbage bags of negativity on us on a regular basis and we get weighed down. Negative people drain our time and energy even when they're not with us.

It's easy to spend 2 hours dreading a 1-hour meeting with a negative person. Combine that with 2 hours of venting after the meeting, and we've just given that person 5 valuable hours of our time. Research has shown that negative people impact our performance at work, our home life and our health.

Not all negative people are destined to be forever negative. People can and do change.

Maybe they will turn a corner and lose their negative nature. Maybe they will be our boss or neighbor one day. Eliminating people from our lives by burning bridges now may be costly in the future. Throughout life we are constantly meeting new people making it impossible to eliminate all negative people. A paradise where negative people are banned, and everyone is giving each other inspiring high fives doesn't exist. There will always be negative people around.

Although they will always be around, we do have control over how much of our time we give to negative people. Spend less time with negative people using the following 3 easy principles. The principles work by asserting how much time we spend around negative people.

3 MINUTE PEOPLE: Toxic. We dread seeing these people. When we interact with them, we instantly feel like we're suffocating under continual truck load after truck load of negative garbage being dumped on us. Politely avoid these people. If we meet them in person, we politely excuse ourselves as we're busy. If they call us, the call goes to voicemail. Save time and energy by keeping communication to messages and emails only with these people.

3 HOUR PEOPLE: Tolerate. The garbage trucks aren't constant but they're still frequent enough for negative garbage to build up. After a few hours we're drowning in negative garbage and need to get out. Limit time with these people. They could be acquaintances that we have dinner with or relatives that we visit. Save time and energy by limiting the time to under 3 hours with these people.

3 DAY PEOPLE: Time out. Like a neighbor who throws a bag of negative garbage over our garden fence every day. We don't notice at first. It happens so gradually that we don't realize. After a few days we take a look around and wonder where all these garbage bags came from! Take a break from these people. They could be colleagues that we work with during the week or family that stay over during the holidays. Save time and energy by taking a lengthy break every 3 days from these people.

2: MORE

Chosen circle. When we're with true friends we laugh louder, live longer and go further faster. Maximize success by spending more time with positive people.

Positive people inspire us to be better, motivate us to achieve our goals and support our success. We feel energized and happy after spending time with them. They encourage us to hit the gym, go for the promotion at work and start our own business. They enrich our lives.

It's important to realize that positive does not mean similar. Too much of the same thing can limit growth. Deliberately seeking out people who think differently provides the different perspectives we need to enhance our growth. Healthy diversity promotes success.

The people we spend most of our time with are the most important people in our lives. Spend more time with positive people. Discover which people are positive by using the following 3 easy principles.

OPTIMISTIC: Pay attention to conversations. Are conversations spent complaining about things or other people? Or, do conversations revolve around being constructive, the good things happening in the world and good things about other people? Positive people are busy looking at the upside of things rather than the downside. They are the people who focus on what they want, rather than what they don't want. They are enthusiastic and push us to pursue our dreams. Positive people are optimistic. Discover positive people and spend more time with them through listening to our conversations.

ACCOUNTABLE: Pay attention to responsibility. When things go wrong is it never their fault? Or, do they tell the truth and work to make it right? Positive people keep their commitments rather than blaming others. They are the people who tell the truth rather than making excuses. They are trustworthy and we know we can count on them when it really matters. Positive people are accountable. Discover positive people and spend more time with them by observing how people behave when things go wrong.

PRODUCTIVE: Pay attention to people's track records. Are they passively waiting for things to happen to them? Or, do they go out and make things happen? Positive people stay focused without getting distracted. They are the people who use time wisely instead of wasting time. They are the people who get real results and motivate us to do the same. Positive people have proven themselves to be productive. Discover positive people and spend more time with them through taking note of people's track records.

1: NEW

Build bridges. New people bring new opportunities. Accelerate learning and grow in new directions through meeting new people.

If we want to achieve great things in life, we need to surround ourselves with great people. It's that simple.

New people bring new knowledge. Every new person that we meet knows something that we don't know. Every new person that we meet is a potential life teacher ready to share their knowledge and wisdom with us. We've all had Aha! moments when a person we've recently met amazes us with a missing piece of information that instantly solves a work or life puzzle. Make more of these moments.

New people bring new perspectives. There are countless ideas out there that we don't even know exist right now. People think differently. New people expose us to new ways of thinking and doing that we never would have thought of before. New people help us solve problems and overcome challenges whilst we help them do the same.

We have the opportunity to learn from every new person that we meet. Great people help us learn faster and grow stronger. Meet new people easily by using the following 3 easy principles.

WHO: Identify the new people to meet. Start with what we are looking for then link this to the type of person who does this. This can be as broad or as specific as we need. If we're looking to develop teamwork, we can link this to team sports such as soccer players. If we're looking for how to be an entrepreneur and start our own business, we can link this to other entrepreneurs who are already running their own businesses.

WHERE: Identify where these people are. Soccer players go to the local soccer club. Entrepreneurs network through regular local meetups held by local entrepreneur organizations. Every activity has a location where people go for the activity. Find this location.

GO: Meet people. Go to the local soccer club and start playing soccer. Go to the local meetups for entrepreneurs. To break the ice when meeting new people find out how they started out in this activity and why they enjoy doing this. Everyone likes to meet new people. Enjoy learning and growing through meeting new people.

GO! SUCCESS WINDOW

Bring out the best. Protect from negative people, promote positive people and meet new people to accelerate learning and growth.

Pro-actively protect time and energy by limiting negative people to 3 minutes, 3 hours or 3 days of time.

Discover positive people by listening to conversations, paying attention when things go wrong and taking note of people's track records.

Meet great new people by going to them and joining in what they're doing.

To create this block for our Success Window simply find a picture that represents positive people and put this picture on a sheet of paper like the example on the next page.

3-2-1-GO! stick this block on our Success Window as the 6th block like below.

<u>SUCCESS WINDOW BLOCK #6: PEOPLE</u>

<u>SUCCESS PLAN: PEOPLE</u>

Easily enjoy being with positive people with 3
Second Success and the following success plans.

<u>GOAL</u>
Less time with negative people

<u>ACTION MOMENT</u>
When with negative people
3-2-1-GO!

<u>ACTION</u>
Spend less time with negative people by
limiting time using the principles:
3 Minutes: Toxic
3 Hours: Tolerate
3 Days: Time out

GOAL

More time with positive people

ACTION MOMENT

When with people
3-2-1-GO!

ACTION

Discover positive people by using the principles:
Optimistic: Listen to conversations
Accountable: When things go wrong
Productive: Track record

GOAL

Meet new people

ACTION MOMENT

Any time
3-2-1-GO!

ACTION

Meet new people using the principles:
Who: Identify who to meet
Where: Identify where they will be
Go: Be where they will be

OPPORTUNITY

"TO HELL WITH CIRCUMSTANCES.

I CREATE OPPORTUNITIES"

BRUCE LEE

Opportunity ignites success after success to empower freedom. Liberating freedom to do what we want, when we want. We have the strength and confidence to transform all challenges into opportunities. We get up and make it happen.

We are committed to developing ourselves without limits. To leverage opportunities that open doors to a life of growth and prosperity. Increase income, decrease working hours and live our dream lives. Regardless of our circumstances, we create opportunities.

Opportunity is like a fruit tree. An apple seed is tiny yet has huge potential. We plant the seed of opportunity now and our life tree grows and grows. Creating opportunities is like watering our life tree. Through regular watering we ensure our tree grows lush green leaves and that it bears ripe fruitful rewards of prosperity and success that increase year on year.

Let's 3-2-1-GO! to enjoying time to thrive, great growth and fulfilling freedom!

TIME

Deliberately purposeful. Calm and clear. Effortlessly focused. Motivated. Creating time to thrive makes all these and more happen.

Use it or lose it. We are born with around 30,000 days. The clock is ticking and every day that passes is gone for good. Lost time can never be regained. We often forget how valuable time is. Like the value of water is only appreciated when there's a drought. We spend a third of our lives sleeping: 10,000 days gone. We spend 5% of our lives eating: 1,500 days gone. We spend over a year of our lives in the bathroom: 500 days gone. After basically staying alive we have a life opportunity of around 18,000 days. Consider childhood, education and work and our life opportunity is now under 10,000 days. Every second, minute, hour and day is priceless. Make the most of every day. Using time wisely is essential for enjoying a life of success.

3: WISE

Wise not waste. Screen time wastes our time every day. Use time wisely through eliminating wasted screen time to create more time.

A survey looking at screen time habits found that on average we spend close to 7 hours a day staring at a screen. Work accounts for part of this but smartphones and TV make up a large part of our screen time. We frequently take a break from one screen to look at another screen. We're all guilty of dual screening at work or whilst watching TV by switching from one screen to another by scrolling through our smartphones. In the morning nearly 80% of us check our smartphones as soon as we wake up with just as many people probably staring at smartphones just before sleeping.

3 out of 4 people agree that they feel they spend too much time looking at a screen. When we spend hours in front of a screen, we're in a seated position for a long time and that's unhealthy. Our bodies lose strength and gain fat because we're not moving. When screens turn us into zoned out zombies our brains aren't being used. Our brains get lazy and this negatively impacts our overall cognitive ability. Whilst we're staring at our smartphone or

watching TV, we're letting opportunity after opportunity pass us by.

The benefits of the digital world enrich our lives, but time is easily stolen by screens when we're unaware of how much time is being hijacked. Take control of screen time to create more time to do what we want by using the following 3 easy principles.

TRACK: What we measure, we improve. Track smartphone use by using built in "Screen Time" features or through an app. Track TV use by making a note of the time spent watching TV. Tracking helps us realize how much screen time we're spending. This awareness makes us conscious of screens wasting our time.

PLAN: Do what we enjoy. Turn free time into valuable time. Evenings and weekends left unplanned are easily hijacked by screens. Plan time with family and friends. Plan time for activities and hobbies. Add these to our daily schedule and calendar.

HABIT: Break free. Most screen time is started by habit. Checking notifications on our smartphones or turning on the TV after work can lead to unintentionally wasting hours and hours. Use 3 Second Success to change these habits by replacing the action of switching on a screen with an action that adds value to our lives. As examples, when we feel the urge to pick up our smartphone instantly 3-2-1-GO! and complete an item on our to do list. When we feel the urge to pick up the TV remote instantly 3-2-1-GO! out for a walk. Replace the habit of switching on screens with productive actions that bring opportunity.

2: NO

Stop sacrificing. We often say yes to things that we don't want to do. Stop sacrificing time and energy. Say no, create more time and feel free.

Saying yes becomes automatic and we end up people pleasing whilst neglecting ourselves. The busy trap catches everyone. We get busier and busier. Before we know it, years have flown by. We all need to keep a roof over our heads and food on the table. We all have life commitments with family and friends. We can't say no to everything and spend the rest of our lives on holiday. Saying no with a positive outcome can be challenging.

Every day at work our email in-boxes are overflowing. They present us with problems that we think we must solve and emails asking us to do things that we don't want to do. Colleagues at work want us to help them with their projects when we've got deadlines of our own to meet. Friends insist that we join them for dinner and drinks when we'd rather stay home, have a long bath and relax.

Every day is like running a race. We run around completing tasks at work and home. Some days we cross the finish line and get to relax but most days we end without the finish line even in sight. Saying yes to things we don't want to do is like adding extra distance to our race. Every time we say yes to something we don't want to do we add an extra mile. The finish line constantly gets pushed further and further away. No wonder we rarely cross the finish line. Our race ends up impossible to finish.

If we reply to all our problem emails, we get more new emails every day as people are happy when we solve their problems. If we help our colleagues all the time at work, they're happy and keep asking for more help. If we say yes to dinner and drinks with friends all the time we don't get to rest or relax. Doing things that we don't want to, just so that we can do even more things that we don't want to, is devastatingly demotivating.

Regular reflection of where our time is going is important. We will always have commitments that give us a race to run every day. We often have choice when we don't realize it. We can choose to make our race longer or shorter. We can re-direct questioning emails to other people or places for their answers. We can maintain a good relationship with colleagues by setting their expectations and helping only when we're free. Friends understand when we need to rest and are happy for us to join them next time. Choosing to decline and say no doesn't have to be negative, it can be positive.

Focus on finishing our race. Help others if our finish line is in sight or after we've finished our own race. Say no positively and make our race shorter by using the following 3 easy principles.

PAUSE: It's easy to automatically reply yes to everything. Pause and think before replying.

OUTCOME: Understand what the consequences are, the advantages and disadvantages, for us and everyone else who is affected by doing this.

NO: Do I want to do this? Now that we know the consequences, we can ask ourselves if we really want to do this. If the answer is no and we don't want to do this, the easiest way to decline is to simply say "I can't" and briefly state why.

1: YES

Live life. Start doing instead of dreaming. Open the floodgates of opportunity with new experiences, fresh ideas and awesome adventures.

Before we were busy. Stuck to screens and stuck in the busy trap. We have freed ourselves from screens and liberated ourselves from the busy trap. We're ready for the powerful potential of saying yes to our dreams.

If we always do what we've always done, we always get what we've always gotten. If we want more, if we want to realize our dreams then we're ready to say yes. Yes, to stepping outside our comfort zone. Yes, to pushing ourselves further. Yes, to feeling fulfilled. We've always wanted to learn piano or guitar. To see the world and travel. To go skydiving. To start our own business. Turn dreams into reality by saying yes and making them happen. What once seemed impossible is now possible.

Say yes to dreams and new experiences that take us beyond our comfort zone using the following 3 easy principles.

COMMIT: Be careful when to say yes. Blindly saying yes to everything will lead to falling back into the busy trap. Be realistic. Check the schedule. If we say yes, we want to be able to commit 100% with our time and energy.

LEARN: New experiences are an opportunity to grow. Same equals stagnant. If we say yes, check that this will be an opportunity for learning and growth.

PEOPLE: New people bring new opportunities. Check who will be there. If we say yes, we want to be with positive people.

GO! SUCCESS WINDOW

Take control of time. Reduce screen time, stop sacrificing time and use newly freed up time to start turning dreams into reality.

Radically reduce screen time wisely by tracking screen time use, planning free time and building productive habits.

Stop and say no to things we don't want to do by pausing to think, understanding the outcome and saying no using "I can't".

Start saying yes only when we can commit 100%, when we can learn and when we'll be with positive people.

To create this block for our Success Window simply find a picture that represents time to thrive and put this picture on a sheet of paper like the example on the next page.

3-2-1-GO! stick this block on our Success Window as the 7th block like below.

SUCCESS WINDOW BLOCK #7: TIME

SUCCESS PLAN: TIME

Easily enjoy time to thrive with 3 Second Success and the following success plans.

GOAL
Create more time

ACTION MOMENT
When about to switch on a screen
3-2-1-GO!

ACTION
Eliminate wasted screen time using the principles:
Track: Measure smartphone and TV usage
Plan: Plan free time
Habit: Build productive habits

GOAL

Say no to things we don't want to do

ACTION MOMENT

When asked to do something
3-2-1-GO!

ACTION

Stop sacrificing using the principles:
Pause: Think before replying
Outcome: Consider the consequences
No: Say "I can't"

GOAL

Say yes to living life

ACTION MOMENT

Planning free time
3-2-1-GO!

ACTION

Realize dreams using the principles:
Commit: Say yes when we can commit 100%
Learn: Check this is a growth opportunity
People: Be with positive people

GROW

Increasing intelligence. Skilled and successful. Feeling fulfilled. Motivated. Growing as a person makes all these and more happen.

Top performers invest in themselves. In sports there are 3 components: training, rest and competition. Athletes who train poorly, perform poorly. Athletes who use regular targeted training that incorporates recreation have the highest performance on game day. If we want to be a winner, we train as a winner. We work on improving ourselves to win the finals and get the gold medals.

Personal growth propels prosperity. Standard education brings standard results. Lifelong learning turns average into advantaged. Go from ordinary to extraordinary. Continual personal growth is essential for enjoying a life of success.

3: LEARN

Sure success. Learn more and earn more. Invest in ourselves to boost professional skills and knowledge.

Real learning for many of us finishes after either high school, college or university. When we start work learning often gets relegated to mandatory training that our job requires us to complete. Learning becomes boring and uninspiring because we're forced by our jobs to do it.

Throughout life we change jobs. A National Longitudinal Survey showed that on average we'll have 12 jobs. These could be promotions or complete career changes. Both require transferable skills and knowledge. Being promoted from a regular job to management and senior management requires a completely different set of skills and knowledge. Going from an employee to a business owner requires a completely different set of skills and knowledge. The ability to transfer skills and knowledge across jobs boosts our success significantly. Focus on continually learning transferable skills and knowledge.

There is literally loads to learn. It's impossible to learn everything. Choosing what to learn and how much of it to learn is important. Focus on the future. Choose skills and knowledge that are transferable to our future promotions and job changes. Target learning to specific areas that are valuable and inspiring.

Data from the Bureau of Labor Statistics shows that those with the highest levels of education have earnings of over triple those with the lowest levels of education. The fastest way to earn more is to grow by learning more. Be smart, choose continual professional development that gets results by using the following 2 easy principles.

INVEST: Set aside time and money every year for professional development. We will see a big return on these investments through increasing income and increasing job satisfaction.

TRANSFERABLE: Evaluate our career path to decide which transferable skills and knowledge to focus on. Example areas are management, strategy, finance and marketing. These are valuable skills in all industries and across all levels from the bottom to the top of an organization.

2: DEVELOP

Personal power. Live to learn. Strategically streamline personal development to achieve rapid results.

We all have powerful potential. The truth is that we struggle to materialize that potential. We initially put in the effort but quickly quit when we don't see results. Once the initial enthusiasm sinks our goals go down with it. It's tempting to jump ship from one goal to the next without ever reaching any goal. Trying to overhaul our entire life at once can feel frustratingly overwhelming.

Throwing in the towel leaves us feeling disappointed and gets us nowhere. Time to change tactics and bring brilliance back to the fight. Time to step back and evaluate our strategy.

Ready, aim, fire. Get the sequence right and we hit targets. If we're chasing an army of goals we tend to fire first. Firing in all directions, we're a loose cannon that misses targets and quickly runs out of ammunition. Focus on one personal development area at a time. This way we focus all our energy towards a single goal and we successfully change an area of our lives. Hitting this goal boosts our confidence and provides the momentum that drives us to change the next area of our lives. Structure personal development to make hitting goals effortless by using the following 3 easy principles.

READY: Making sure our gun is clean and in top shape. That we're loaded with ammunition. Readiness is planning our personal development to optimize results. Scheduling regular personal development time and being loaded with enthusiastic energy.

AIM: Knowing what our target is. Having our gun pointed directly at what we want to hit. Knowing what we're shooting for and being properly aligned to hit it. Aim is focusing on a single clearly defined, measurable and time limited goal.

FIRE: Pulling the trigger and hitting the target. Firing is executing our personal development plan and intentionally making it happen.

1: ENJOY

Work hard, play harder. Fresh ideas and originality are born out of play and creativity. Enrich life with creative leisure to turn stress into smiles.

Disconnecting from work and reconnecting with ourselves brings benefits. A mind full of targets and deadlines never rests. The constant demands of work can build up to burning out.

Studies have confirmed that creative hobbies immensely impact our lives. An increase of 15% to 30% in work performance. Enhanced confidence. Improved memory and cognition. Longer life expectancy. Feeling fulfilled. Creative hobbies play a vital role in our health and happiness.

Relax and refresh with creative hobbies. Wipe away work. Start with a blank canvas. Get creative. We already have inspiring ideas for hobbies. Look back in life and find what we enjoyed in the past. Look inside and find what we always wanted to do but never got chance. Many of us enjoy making music, cooking and art. From rock star to classical pianist, baking cookies to gourmet meals, drawing stick people to painting masterpieces. Choose hobbies that enrich life by using the following 2 easy principles.

CREATIVE: Thinking test. Does this hobby make us think? Is this hobby a challenge? Increase intelligence with hobbies that inspire.

FUN: Smile test. Does this hobby make us smile? Enjoying hobbies is essential for enriching life.

GO! SUCCESS WINDOW

Invest in inspiration. Mix professional and personal development with creative leisure to enjoy sky-high smiles.

Target continual professional development towards transferable skills to reap rewards when opportunities open.

Ready, aim, fire at a single personal development area at a time to secure success.

Choose creative hobbies that get us thinking and bring smiles to reset and feel refreshed.

To create this block for our Success Window simply find a picture that represents growth and put this picture on a sheet of paper like the example on the next page.

3-2-1-GO! stick this block on our Success Window as the 8th block like below.

<u>SUCCESS WINDOW BLOCK #8: GROW</u>

<u>SUCCESS PLAN: GROW</u>

Easily enjoy great growth with 3 Second Success and the following success plans.

<u>GOAL</u>
Continual professional development

<u>ACTION MOMENT</u>
Career planning
3-2-1-GO!

<u>ACTION</u>
Earn more using the principles:
Invest: Time and money
Transferable: Skills and knowledge

GOAL

Personal development

ACTION MOMENT

Personal development planning
3-2-1-GO!

ACTION

Get rapid results using the principles:
Ready: Schedule regular time
Aim: Focus on one goal
Fire: Take action

GOAL

Creative hobbies

ACTION MOMENT

Planning free time
3-2-1-GO!

ACTION

Enrich life using the principles:
Creative: Thinking test
Fun: Smile test

FREEDOM

Increasing income. Pursuing our passion. Financially free. Motivated. Finding focus makes all these and more happen.

Imagine we have a huge empty swimming pool in the sunshine. We go get the garden hose and start filling up our pool. It's slow going, this is going to take forever. The pool is our net worth and the garden hose is our income from our job. It'll take decades to be able to kick back and enjoy the pool. Let's work this out. We can turn the tap on further to increase the flow. This is like getting bonuses for being productive at work. We can get a bigger hose. This is like getting a better paying job. We can get more hoses. This is like building additional income streams. Fast-track filling our pool and we're free to jump in whenever we want. Focusing on financial freedom is essential for enjoying a life of success.

3: FOCUS

Rising reputation. Get things done. Work effectively to bank bonuses and be noted for promotion.

Meeting after meeting, endless emails and plenty of paperwork. We attend all meetings, reply to all emails promptly and get documents done by the deadline. We're efficient. The problem is that efficient does not equal effective. We're efficient at meetings, efficient at emails and efficient at paperwork but efficiency alone doesn't get the important work done. This ground-level focus keeps us busy but also keeps us at ground-level. Gain perspective by climbing the mountain and surveying the whole landscape. We soon see that our scurrying around at ground-level has very little impact on the landscape. At this altitude we can see for miles. We can see what everyone is doing and what will have the largest impact towards changing the landscape. With an overview of everything we can choose to focus on important work that will have the greatest impact on our goals. By doing this we instantly go from average to outstanding.

Be effective at work by finding and focusing on important work by using the following 3 easy principles.

PURPOSE: Does this task need to be done? Does it work towards our goals? Eliminate pointless tasks.

PRIORITIZE: Order tasks by importance and urgency. Start at the top. Work on a task until complete then move on to the next task.

PRODUCTIVE: Is this an efficient way to do this task? Make difficult and time-consuming tasks easier and faster to complete by changing how we work.

2: MONEY

Increase income. Get paid more. Create conversations that make more money and produce promotions.

When was the last time we checked our value? Are we getting paid above or below our value? How can we increase our value and get paid more?

Everybody has a market value. This is the value of our skills and knowledge to employers. Know our value. Regularly review local job advertisements. Compare what is being offered on the job market for our current job and the job that will be the next step in our career. Include other benefits and perks that employers offer. Health insurance, vacations, pension plans and so on. Look at the whole package.

Aim to be paid above our market value. Aim to increase our market value through professional development and promotion. Be prepared to change jobs to a new employer to realize our increasing value.

Directly asking for a pay raise or promotion can feel awkward. Awkward for us and awkward for our manager. When and how we ask determines the difference between sink or success.

When our employer hits hard times, it's best to focus on being effective and building up a portfolio of evidence that demonstrates our value. When business is booming, we have the perfect opportunity to climb our career ladder. Monthly reviews and annual reviews are ideal times to discuss pay and promotions.

Working with our manager and taking their advice goes a long way towards realizing our goals. Discussing pay raises and promotions leads to managers providing constructive feedback about us and the way we work. Use these learning opportunities to show that we utilize feedback and that we have what they are looking for.

Switching employers can bring new opportunities. Pay raises and promotions can be larger and faster. The prospects at a new employer can be much more than where we are currently.

Regular market valuation brings confidence to performance review meetings and interviews. We know what we're worth. Having the facts and figures to back this up are essential to negotiating pay raises and promotions. Get paid more and promoted faster by using the following 3 easy principles.

PAY: Our employer may have a structure where pay raises are automatic when we hit targets or unstructured where we ask for a pay raise. Either way the fastest way to get a pay raise is to discuss this with our manager. Asking for a pay raise is easy when we ask the right way. Ask our manager "A pay raise would be great, how can we make that happen?". This creates an open conversation. An open conversation that directly leads to discussing what actions are needed to get a pay raise, when this will happen and how much our pay raise will be.

PROMOTE: The fastest way to get a promotion is to discuss this with our manager. Ask our manager "A promotion to (insert job title here) would be great, how can we make that happen?". This creates an open conversation. A good manager will provide feedback about what we need to do to get the promotion we want. It may be developing hard skills like analysis or soft skills like communication. Act on this feedback and clearly prove that we're the person for promotion. When positions open up this makes sure that we're first in line for promotion.

PROSPECT: When pay and promotion are limited it's time to prospect. Apply and interview for jobs. Look for a new employer. Prospecting is about choice and options. When we have options, we're in a strong position to negotiate pay raises and promotions.

1: BUSINESS

Money magnet. Businesses can have unlimited earning potential. Bringing business ideas to life fast-tracks financial freedom.

Driving home, grocery shopping and the middle of the night. New business ideas launch into our lives all the time. Most are crazy but some sparkle. Brainstorming business ideas is like mining diamonds. Everything starts with a bang. Blowing up rocks with dynamite is like new business ideas exploding into our thoughts. Sorting through the stones to separate the waste from the rough diamonds is like picking out the best business ideas. Cutting and polishing the diamonds is like researching and proving the potential of the best business ideas.

Feel true freedom by starting a successful business by using the following 3 easy principles.

PASSION: Brainstorm business ideas that ignite passion. Passion is enthusiasm. Turn rocks into diamonds. Create business ideas that spark determination and drive.

POTENTIAL: Successful businesses have the potential to grow and grow. Uncut diamonds are worth next to nothing. Cut and polished diamonds are worth millions. Do the research and prove the potential.

PLAN: Prosperity is built on planning. Build our mine in the wrong place and we only have rocks and sand. Build our mine in the right place and we unearth a river of continuously flowing diamonds. Use business planning to build a business that prospers.

Start a business. Be successful:

3-2-1-GO! to 3Second**Success**.com/**business**

Invest. Be successful:

3-2-1-GO! to 3Second**Success**.com/**invest**

GO! SUCCESS WINDOW

Rising through the ranks. Focus on increasing income at work and start a business to feel freedom.

Find and focus on important work to build a reputation for being effective.

Know what we're worth and openly approach pay raise and promotion discussions to get paid more and more.

Start a business to transform ideas into income.

To create this block for our Success Window simply find a picture that represents freedom and put this picture on a sheet of paper like the example on the next page.

3-2-1-GO! stick this block on our Success Window as the 9th block like below.

SUCCESS WINDOW BLOCK #9: FREEDOM

SUCCESS PLAN: FREEDOM

Easily enjoy fulfilling freedom with 3 Second Success and the following success plans.

GOAL
Be effective

ACTION MOMENT
Completing tasks
3-2-1-GO!

ACTION
Focus on important work using the principles:
Purpose: Does this need to be done?
Prioritize: Is this important or urgent?
Productive: Can this be done easier and faster?

GOAL

Increase income

ACTION MOMENT

Monthly and annual reviews
3-2-1-GO!

ACTION

Get pay raises and promotions using the principles:

Pay: Ask manager how to raise pay

Promote: Ask manager how to be promoted

Prospect: Look for new jobs

GOAL

Feel freedom

ACTION MOMENT

Now
3-2-1-GO!

ACTION

Start a successful business using the principles:

Passion: Brainstorm

Potential: Research

Plan: Create a business plan

3 SECOND **SUCCESS**

THE **MOMENT** YOU FEEL THAT YOU
WANT TO TAKE ACTION
TOWARDS **A GOAL**
INSTANTLY **START COUNTING** DOWN

3-2-1-GO!

ON GO! **MOVE** AND **TAKE ACTION!**

STRENGTH: **BE STRONG**

CONFIDENCE: **BE RESPECTED**

OPPORTUNITY: **BE SUCCESSFUL**

MASTER MOTIVATION. BE SUCCESSFUL!

3Second**Success**.com

START A BUSINESS. BE SUCCESSFUL!

3Second**Success**.com/**business**

INVEST. BE SUCCESSFUL!

3Second**Success**.com/**invest**

www.ingramcontent.com/pod-product-compliance
Lightning Source LLC
Chambersburg PA
CBHW051108050726
47592CB00002B/729